King size
Quilt 73 x 94

1001

PATCHWORK

DESIGNS

MAGGIE MALONE

 Sterling Publishing Co., Inc.   New York

ACKNOWLEDGMENTS

I would like to thank my daughter, Kelly, for the many hours she spent helping me prepare this book. Without her assistance I could never have completed the manuscript on time.

And a thank you to my mother, Ann DeWeese, for her patience in putting up with papers and books sprawling all over her house.

Library of Congress Cataloging in Publication Data

Malone, Maggie, 1942–
    1001 patchwork designs.

    Bibliography: p.
    Includes indexes.
    1. Patchwork—Patterns.   I. Title.
II. Title: One thousand one patchwork designs.
III. Title: One thousand and one patchwork
designs.
TT835.M347   746.46'041   81-85037
ISBN 0-8069-5460-4   AACR2
ISBN 0-8069-5461-2 (lib. bdg.)
ISBN 0-8069-7604-7 (pbk.)

Copyright © 1982 by Sterling Publishing Co., Inc.
Two Park Avenue, New York, N.Y. 10016
Distributed in Australia by Oak Tree Press Co., Ltd.
P.O. Box K514 Haymarket, Sydney 2000, N.S.W.
Distributed in the United Kingdom by Blandford Press
Link House, West Street, Poole, Dorset BH15 1LL, England
Distributed in Canada by Oak Tree Press Ltd.
% Canadian Manda Group, 215 Lakeshore Boulevard East
Toronto, Ontario M5A 3W9
Manufactured in the United States of America
All rights reserved

Contents

Introduction

Quiltmaking's continued popularity attests to its ability to offer something for everyone. Perhaps you made a quilt for the warmth and charm it gives a room. Or for the opportunity it gives you to put your own personal stamp on your surroundings. Or the satisfaction derived when you present a quilt to someone special, made to suit their tastes and decor. It's a wonderful creative outlet for experiments in color and design. It may be your form of tranquillizer, soothing away the day's tensions with each stitch you take. Or you may enjoy the challenge of competition, testing your design ability and workmanship against all other entrants.

Every stage of making a quilt has something to offer. Perhaps you like the planning stage, choosing just the right colors and tracking down the fabrics. Or the piecing, watching the colors interact and bringing the design alive beneath your fingers. Or perhaps you prefer the quilting stage, taking the tiny, perfect stitches needed to make a masterpiece quilt.

For whatever reason you make a quilt, there are shortcuts and speed techniques to get you over the drudgery to the part you really love to do. To the purists a quilt is a quilt only when made from 100% cotton, with every stitch taken by hand, and the quilting stitches 20 to the inch. I've often marvelled at the beauty and intricacy of the quilts created by hand —and at the patience required to execute them.

However, not every quilt is intended to be a masterpiece. And some of us don't sew very well by hand, and really don't want to take the time to learn, especially when we have our speedy little sewing machines to do the work for us. A quilt made on the sewing machine can be just as beautiful as those done by hand.

In my classes I try to give my students a thorough grounding in the basics, then I encourage them to experiment. I don't lay down hard and fast dos and don'ts. The correct method is whatever method works for you to achieve results of which you can be proud. I believe in simplifying. Quiltmaking is a simple craft, but as with every other craft, there are those who attempt to imbue it with mystery and obscurity, which does nothing but frighten the beginner, for one can never hope to achieve the artificial standards set up by those in the "inner circle."

This book contains 1,001 patterns, but it is by no means all-inclusive. For the most part, I've tried to stick with the simple geometric designs that are easy to draw up, but there are more difficult patterns for the experienced quilter. The designs are grouped according to the number of patches, making up the block, such as 4-patch, 9-patch, and so on. Each one is clearly marked with graph lines to enable you to scale the block to any size desired. An additional benefit is that as you work with the patterns in this book you will learn to recognize the underlying construction of any block you see.

You will also note that within each group many of the pattern pieces are interchangeable. For instance, if you draft a pattern for a 9-patch block, you can also make Patience 9-patch and Red Cross with those same pattern pieces. When you draft the Hourglass pattern, you can also make Calico Puzzle, Shoofly, Snowball, Friendship Star, Box, and several others, by using the same pattern pieces.

The sections on pattern drafting explain how to scale a block to any size. Whether you work by hand or with the sewing machine, there are techniques that can be of use to you in achieving smooth, perfectly aligned blocks.

With the methods given here you can adapt and combine patterns to create truly unique quilts.

METRIC EQUIVALENCY CHART

CONVERTING INCHES TO CENTIMETRES AND YARDS TO METRES

mm — millimetres   cm — centimetres   m — metres

INCHES INTO MILLIMETRES AND CENTIMETRES
(SLIGHTLY ROUNDED FOR YOUR CONVENIENCE)

inches	mm		cm	inches	cm	inches	cm
⅛	3mm			7	18	29	73.5
¼	6mm			8	20.5	30	76
⅜	10mm	or	1cm	9	23	31	78.5
½	13mm	or	1.3cm	10	25.5	32	81.5
⅝	15mm	or	1.5cm	11	28	33	84
¾	20mm	or	2cm	12	30.5	34	86.5
⅞	22mm	or	2.2cm	13	33	35	89
1	25mm	or	2.5cm	14	35.5	36	91.5
1¼	32mm	or	3.2cm	15	38	37	94
1½	38mm	or	3.8cm	16	40.5	38	96.5
1¾	45mm	or	4.5cm	17	43	39	99
2	50mm	or	5cm	18	46	40	102
2½	65mm	or	6.3cm	19	48.5	41	104
3	75mm	or	7.5cm	20	51	42	107
3½	90mm	or	9cm	21	53.5	43	109
4	100mm	or	10cm	22	56	44	112
4½	115mm	or	11.5cm	23	58.5	45	115
5	125mm	or	12.5cm	24	61	46	117
5½	140mm	or	14cm	25	63.5	47	120
6	150mm	or	15cm	26	66	48	122
				27	68.5	49	125
				28	71	50	127

YARDS TO METRES
(SLIGHTLY ROUNDED FOR YOUR CONVENIENCE)

YARDS	METRES	YARDS	METRES	YARDS	METRES	YARDS	METRES	YARDS	METRES
⅛	0.15	2⅛	1.95	4⅛	3.80	6⅛	5.60	8⅛	7.45
¼	0.25	2¼	2.10	4¼	3.90	6¼	5.75	8¼	7.55
⅜	0.35	2⅜	2.20	4⅜	4.00	6⅜	5.85	8⅜	7.70
½	0.50	2½	2.30	4½	4.15	6½	5.95	8½	7.80
⅝	0.60	2⅝	2.40	4⅝	4.25	6⅝	6.10	8⅝	7.90
¾	0.70	2¾	2.55	4¾	4.35	6¾	6.20	8¾	8.00
⅞	0.80	2⅞	2.65	4⅞	4.50	6⅞	6.30	8⅞	8.15
1	0.95	3	2.75	5	4.60	7	6.40	9	8.25
1⅛	1.05	3⅛	2.90	5⅛	4.70	7⅛	6.55	9⅛	8.35
1¼	1.15	3¼	3.00	5¼	4.80	7¼	6.65	9¼	8.50
1⅜	1.30	3⅜	3.10	5⅜	4.95	7⅜	6.75	9⅜	8.60
1½	1.40	3½	3.20	5½	5.05	7½	6.90	9½	8.70
1⅝	1.50	3⅝	3.35	5⅝	5.15	7⅝	7.00	9⅝	8.80
1¾	1.60	3¾	3.45	5¾	5.30	7¾	7.10	9¾	8.95
1⅞	1.75	3⅞	3.55	5⅞	5.40	7⅞	7.20	9⅞	9.05
2	1.85	4	3.70	6	5.50	8	7.35	10	9.15

Creating
With Color

Attic Window

Two ways to use color for a completely different quilt.

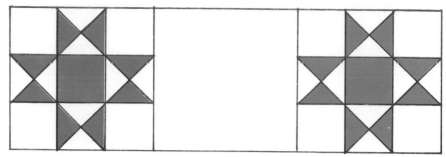

Set with alternate plain blocks.

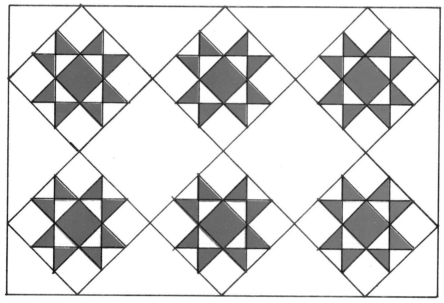

Diagonal set gives the Ohio Star pattern a new look. Lattice strips could also be used between the blocks.

Set with lattice strips.

Blocks set solid.

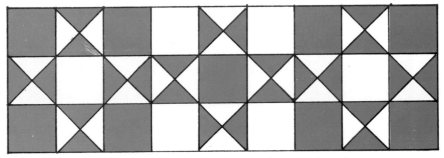

Pattern becomes a form of Shoofly when dark and light colors are alternated from block to block.

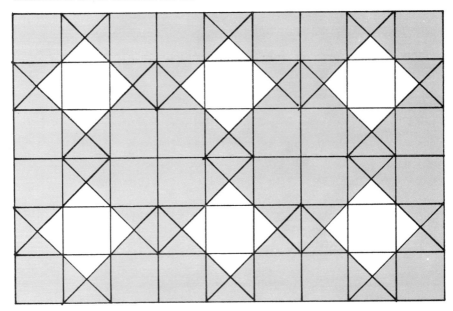

Ohio Star pattern—the color sequence has been changed so that a whole new pattern emerges.

Windblown Square

Set with alternate plain blocks, the design creates an
entirely different quilt than when set solid.

12

Twist

Octagon or Snowball

Snowball and Twist become Caning.

One-and-Two-Patch Designs

1 Rail Fence I

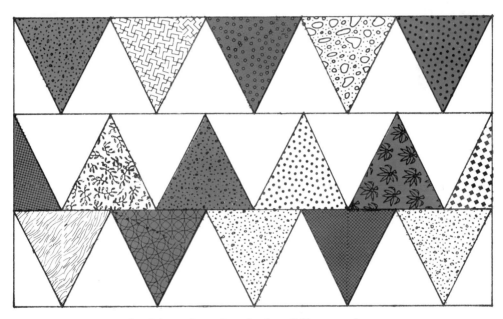

2 Rail Fence II, each of the color triangles is a different color.

3 Basket Weave

15

4 London Stairs I

5 Country Charm

6 Tumbler

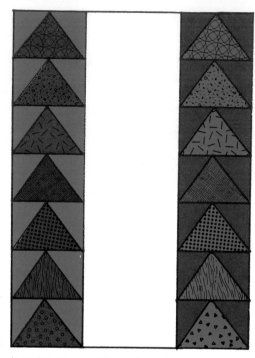

7 Wild Goose Chase I

8 Tree Everlasting I

9 Triangles I

10 Honeycomb

11 Spools

12 Clamshell

13 Thousand Pyramids

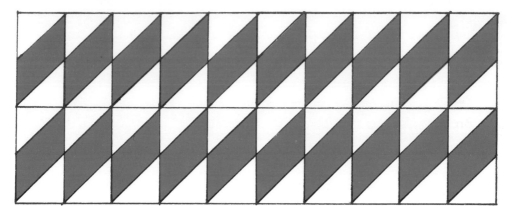

14 Streak of Lightning I

15 Brick

16 Triangles II

Green
Red
Yellow
Purple
Brown

17 Diamond Flower Basket

18 Land of Pharaoh

19 Magic Squares

20 Rail Fence III

21 Grandmother's Flower Garden

22 Spools II

23 Honeycomb II

24 Baby Blocks

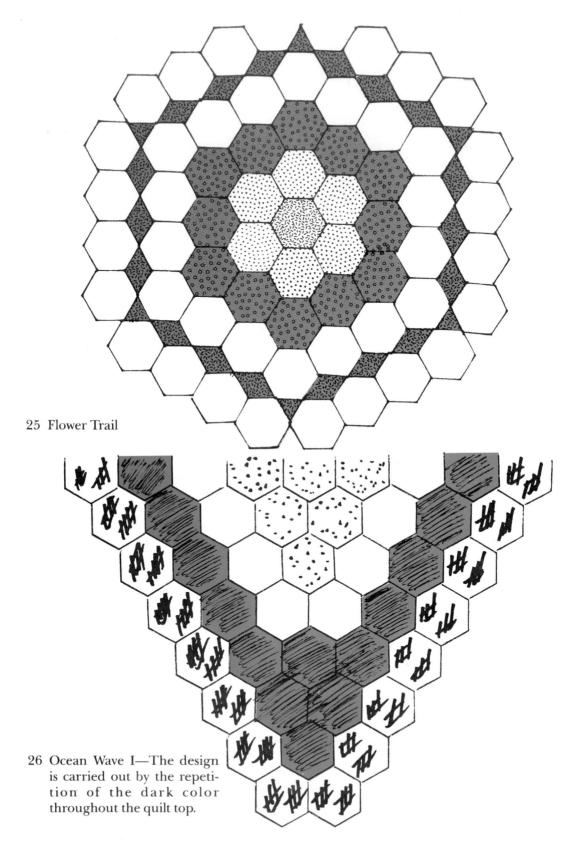

25 Flower Trail

26 Ocean Wave I—The design
is carried out by the repeti-
tion of the dark color
throughout the quilt top.

Nine-Patch Designs

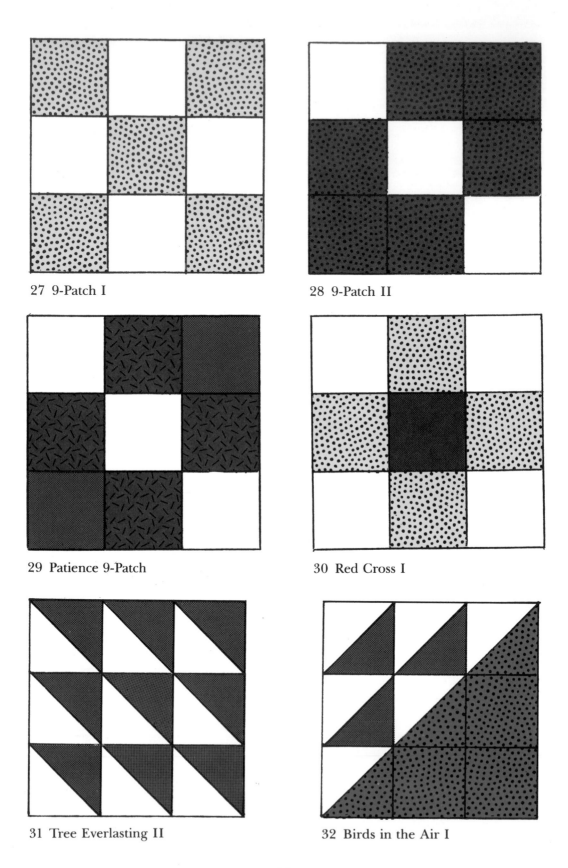

27 9-Patch I

28 9-Patch II

29 Patience 9-Patch

30 Red Cross I

31 Tree Everlasting II

32 Birds in the Air I

The major advantage of being able to draft a pattern is the flexibility it allows you in designing a quilt. For a sampler quilt, you can scale all the blocks to the same size. You might want to make a large medallion type of quilt, and with a little knowledge of pattern construction, it's a simple matter to draft the pattern up in size.

Another advantage is that you know it's accurate. Most printed patterns are off slightly, with the result that the finished pieces will not fit together properly. This is usually caused by distortion in the printing process, but there are honest mistakes made, too.

If you are using the patterns in this book you will note that most of them have graph lines underlying the design areas. This allows you to see how many squares make up each block, and the divisions within each square.

At this point you should decide how large to make the finished block. I don't like working with fractions, so I always try to scale the block in even numbers. For example, a 9-patch block would be drawn with each square equalling 3″ or 4″, giving a finished block of 9″ or 12″. But if I were to make this an 8″ block, I'd be dealing with fractions throughout.

Now to muddy the waters a bit. In drafting patterns I've found that a basic 9-patch can be further broken down by dividing each square in half or into thirds, and in some instances into fourths. In these cases, you can't figure final block size from the basic 9-patch, but must deal with the total number of squares in the block.

The following diagrams illustrate each pattern type and how to arrive at a final block size.

Basic 9-Patch

Square = Final Block Size

1″ = 3″ block
2″ = 6″ block
3″ = 9″ block
4″ = 12″ block
5″ = 15″ block
6″ = 18″ block

33 Hourglass I

34 Calico Puzzle

35 Attic Window

36 Contrary Wife I

37 Friendship Star

38 9-Patch Star I

39 Box

40 Formal Garden I

41 Snowball I

42 Snowball Variation

43 Sawtooth I

44 Maple Leaf I

9-Patch
Divided in Half

1″ = 6″ block
2″ = 12″ block
3″ = 15″ block
4″ = 24″ block

9-Patch
Divided into Thirds

1″ = 9″ block
2″ = 18″ block

9-Patch Divided into Fourths

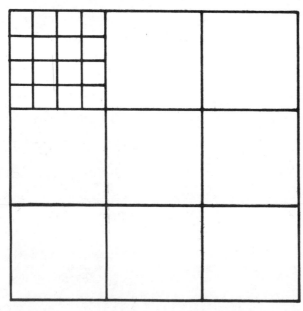

1″ = 12″ block
2″ = 24″ block

45 Shoofly I

46 Cactus Bud

47 Practical Orchard

48 Clown's Choice

49 Malvina's Chain

50 Letter-X I

51 Buckwheat

52 Card Tricks

53 Color Wheel

54 Arkansas Snowflake

55 Time & Tide

56 Nonesuch

57 Mississippi

58 Variable Star

59 Ohio Star

60 Country Farm

61 Prosperity

62 Card Basket

31

63 Braced Star I

64 Rhode Island

65 Braced Star II

66 Stellie

67 Twin Star

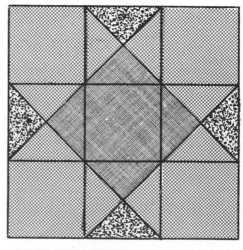

68 Ohio Star Variation

32

69 Modern Tulip

70 Turkey Tracks I

71 Tassel Plant

72 New Jersey

73 Flower Basket I

74 Cactus Basket

75 Goblet

76 Wings

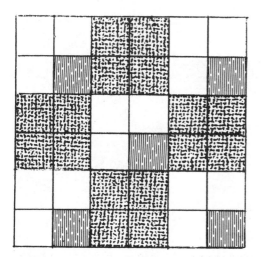

77 Pussy in the Corner

78 Pennsylvania I

79 Homeward Bound

80 New Album I

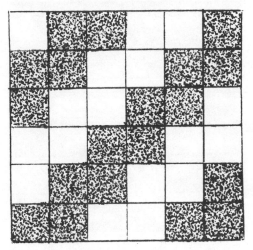

81 Streak of Lightning II

82 Postage Stamp

83 Patience Corner

84 Domino I

85 9-Patch Plaid

86 Hourglass II

87 Broken Sugar Bowl

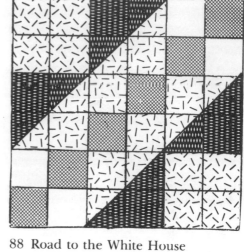

88 Road to the White House

89 Jacob's Ladder I

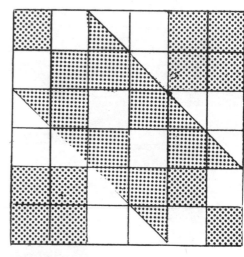

90 Rocky Road to California

91 Railroad I

92 Jacob's Ladder II

93 Churn Dash I

94 Wrench

95 Grecian Design

96 Greek Cross I

97 Cups & Saucers

98 Prairie Queen I

99 Weathervane Variation

100 9-Patch III

101 Lucky Clover

102 Garden Path I

103 Aunt Sukey's Choice

104 Weathervane

105 Capital T

106 Illinois

107 Imperial T

108 Vermont

109 Sawtooth Patchwork

110 Aunt Vinah's Favorite

111 Saint George's Cross

112 Indian Puzzle

113 All Kinds

114 Love in a Mist

115 Wood Lily

116 Spider Legs

40

117 Winged Square I

118 Cut Glass Dish

119 Steps to the Altar I

120 Birds in the Air II

121 Corn & Beans

122 Cat's Cradle

123 Sawtooth II

124 Squash Blossom

125 Rosebud I

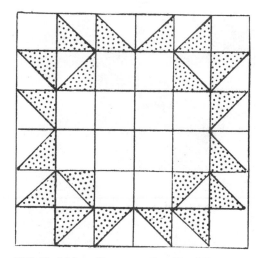

126 Robbing Peter to Pay Paul I

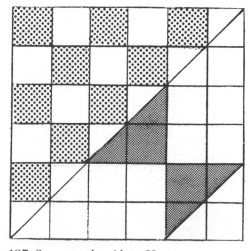

127 Steps to the Altar II

128 Silver Lane

129 Mother's Delight

130 St. Louis

131 Optical Illusion

132 Sunbeam

133 Barbara Bannister Star

134 All Hallows

135 Checkerboard

136 Courthouse Square

137 9-Patch IV

138 Arbor Window

139 Jefferson City

140 Sawtooth Patch

141 Union Square I

142 Union Square II

143 Contrary Wife II

144 Arizona

145 Star Gardner

146 Wyoming Valley

147 Square Dance

148 Kelly's Block

149 54-40 or Fight

150 Bird of Paradise

151 Doris's Delight

152 Rosebuds

153 Strawberry Basket I

154 Strawberry Basket II

155 Basket I

156 Flower Pot I

157 Birthday Cake

158 Grandmother's Basket

159 Queen Victoria's Crown

160 Mrs. Cleveland's Choice

161 9-Patch Frame

162 W.C.T.U.

163 Boxes

164 Handy Andy I

165 Flower Garden Path

166 Spider Web I

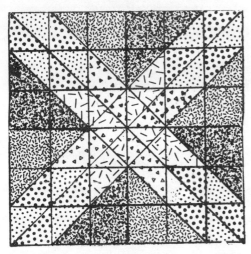

167 Patch as Patch Can

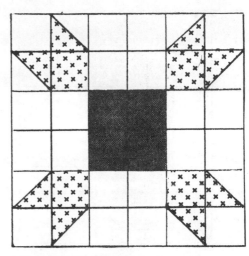

168 Tulip Lady Fingers I

169 Cross Variation

170 Swing in the Center I

171 Winged Square II

172 Dover Block

173 Morning

174 Four Winds

175 Jackknife

176 Storm Signal

177 Grandmother's Own I

178 Arkansas Star

179 Sweet Gum Leaf

180 Battlegrounds

181 Arkansas Traveller I

182 Wheeling 9-Patch

183 Flutterwheel

184 Sugar Loaf

185 Flying Dutchman

186 Spools III

187 Letter-X II

188 Pine Tree I

189 Annapolis Patch

190 Pinwheel Star I

191 Nosegay I

192 Eight-Point Star I

193 Walking Triangles

194 Bow

195 9-Patch Star II

196 Fern Berry

197 Ranger's Pride

198 Combination Star

199 Air Castle

200 Entertaining Motions

201 Claws

202 Eccentric Star

203 Sparkler

204 North Carolina Star

205 Triangle Puzzle

206 Indianapolis

207 Butterfly I

208 Mrs. Morgan's Choice

209 Turnabout-T

210 Rolling Pinwheel

211 Double Pinwheel I

212 South Dakota

213 Double Tulip

214 Tulip I

215 Wheeling Triangles

216 Exea's Star

217 No Name Patch

218 Maple Leaf II

219 Ribbons I

220 Century of Progress I

221 T-Quartette

222 Merry Kite

223 Christmas Star

224 Morning Star I

225 Workbox

226 Crazy Quilt Bouquet

227 Mexican Star

228 Magnolia Bud

229 Double Sawtooth I

230 Grandmother's Puzzle

231 Hayes's Corners

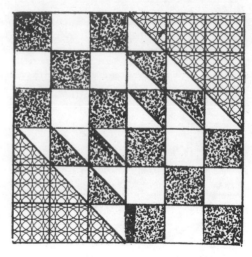

232 Battle of the Alamo

233 Tic Tac Toe

234 English Ivy

235 Ozark Maple Leaf

236 California

237 Hill & Valley

238 Virginia Reel

239 Fancy Flowers

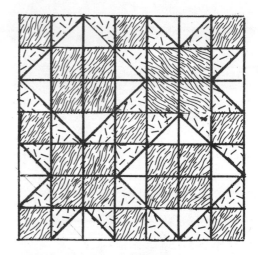

240 Road to California I

241 Four Queens

242 Peacock

61

243 Swing in the Center II

244 Cats & Mice I

245 Conventional Block

246 Flutterbye

247 Rolling Stone

248 Single Wedding **Ring I**

249 H-Block

250 Shooting Star I

251 Pineapple

252 Arab Tent

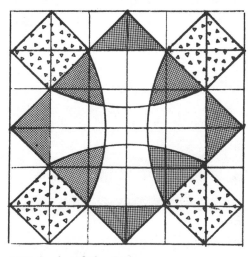

253 Lady of the Lake

254 Kitchen Woodbox

255 Star & Crescent

256 Gretchen

257 Hopscotch

258 Night & Day

259 Guiding Star

260 Temperance Tree

261 Four-H

262 London Stairs II

263 Twisting Star

264 Colonial Rose

265 Ladies Wreath I

266 Dumbell Block

267 Darting Bird

268 Gentleman's Fancy

269 Four Crowns

270 Double-X I

271 Triplet

272 Pine Tree II

273 Montana

274 Golda, Gem Star

275 Golden Gate

276 London Roads I

277 London Roads II

278 Chain & Hourglass

279 Farmer's Puzzle

280 Turkey Tracks II

281 Santa Fe

282 Continental I

283 Arkansas I

284 Alabama

285 Double 9-Patch

286 New 9-Patch

287 Mixed T

288 Blue Blazes

289 Patchwork Posy

290 Mollie's Choice

291 Premium Star

292 St. Louis Star

293 Tile Puzzle

294 Log Cabin I

295 Bear's Den

296 Dolly Madison Star

297 Puss in the Corner I

298 Album I

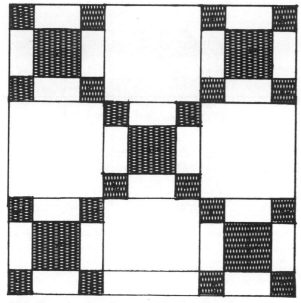

299 Puss in the Corner II

300 Building Blocks

301 Hand Weave

302 Joseph's Coat I

303 Crosspatch

304 Quadrille

305 City Streets

306 Wandering Lanes

307 Dublin Chain

308 Garden Path II

309 Mother's Dream I

310 Little Rock Block

311 Merry-Go-Round I

312 At the Square

313 9-Patch V

314 Annie's Choice

315 Shooting Star II

316 Double Pyramid

317 Mosaic I

318 Pinwheel Askew

319 Mosaic #9

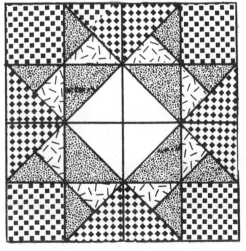

320 Missouri Star I

Four-Patch Designs

2″ = 4″ block
3″ = 6″ block
4″ = 8″ block
5″ = 10″ block
6″ = 12″ block
7″ = 14″ block
8″ = 16″ block
9″ = 18″ block

4-Patch

4-Patch
Divided in Half

2″ = 8″ block
3″ = 12″ block
4″ = 16″ block
5″ = 20″ block

4-Patch
Divided into Fourths

1″ = 8″ block
2″ = 16″ block
3″ = 24″ block

321 4-Patch

322 Pinwheel II

323 Cotton Reel

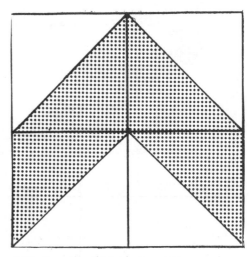

324 Streak of Lightning III

325 Birds ın the Air III

326 Big Dipper

78

327 Broken Dishes I

328 Broken Pinwheel

329 Double Pinwheel II

330 Turnstile

331 Southern Belle

332 Devil's Puzzle

333 Periwinkle

334 Crossed Canoes

335 Laced Star

336 Southern Star

337 Shoemaker's Puzzle

338 Endless Chain

339 Red Cross II

340 Borrow & Return

341 Twist & Turn

342 Stars & Stripes

343 State of Ohio

344 Rosebud II

345 16-Patch

346 Scot's Plaid

347 4-Patch Variation

348 Rainbow Flower

349 Shadow Box

350 Jewel I

351 Susannah I

352 Susannah II

353 Susannah III

354 Art Square

355 New Album II

356 Coxey's Camp

357 Album II

358 Shoofly II

359 King's Crown I

360 Economy

361 Twelve Triangles

362 Right & Left

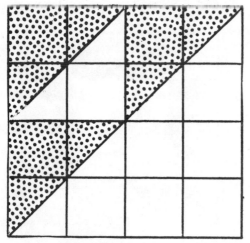

363 Birds in the Air IV

364 Flock

365 Sawtooth III

366 Northern Lights

367 Hovering Hawks

368 Anvil

369 Eight-Point Star II

370 Evening Star

371 Stars & Squares

372 Star I

373 Tippecanoe & Tyler Too

374 8-Hands Around

375 The Seasons

376 Mother's Choice I

377 Pointed Tile

378 Indian Star

379 King's X

380 Primrose Path I

381 Mrs. Taft's Choice

382 Rocky Mountain Puzzle

383 Double-X II

384 Double-X III

385 Old Maid's Puzzle

386 Crosses & Losses

387 Cross in a Cross

388 Circle in a Frame

389 Small Business

390 Autumn Tints

391 Balkan Puzzle

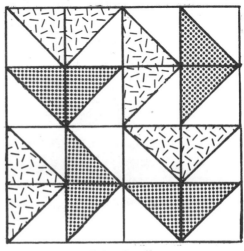

392 Return of the Swallows

393 Missouri Star II

394 Martha Washington Star

395 Mother's Choice II

396 Star II

397 Missouri Star III

398 Star III

399 Album Star

400 Northumberland Star

401 French Star

402 Mexican Cross I

403 Fox Chase

404 Wild Geese

405 Trailing Star

406 Ribbon Star

407 Clay's Choice

408 Pinwheel Star II

409 Pierced Star

410 Missouri Daisy

411 Nelson's Victory

412 Windows (diagonal set)

413 Windmill I

414 Arkansas Crossroads

415 Road to Oklahoma I

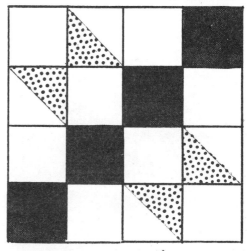

416 Road to Oklahoma II

417 Job's Troubles

418 World Without End

419 Kaleidoscope I

420 World's Fair

421 Key West Star

422 Key West Beauty

423 Aunt Eliza's Star

424 Peaceful Hours

425 No Name

426 Pennsylvania II

427 Arabic Lattice

428 Winding Walk

429 Swallow

430 Seesaw

431 Spinner

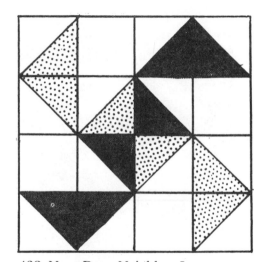

432 Next Door Neighbor I

433 Aircraft

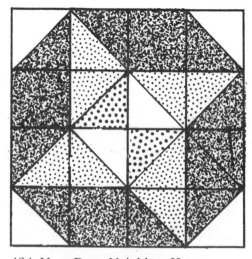

434 Next Door Neighbor II

435 Cats & Mice II

436 Skyrocket

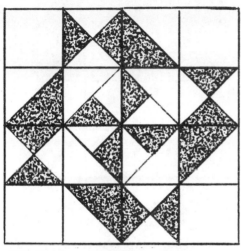

437 Catch as You Can

438 Mosaic II

439 Grandmother's Own

440 Indian Puzzle

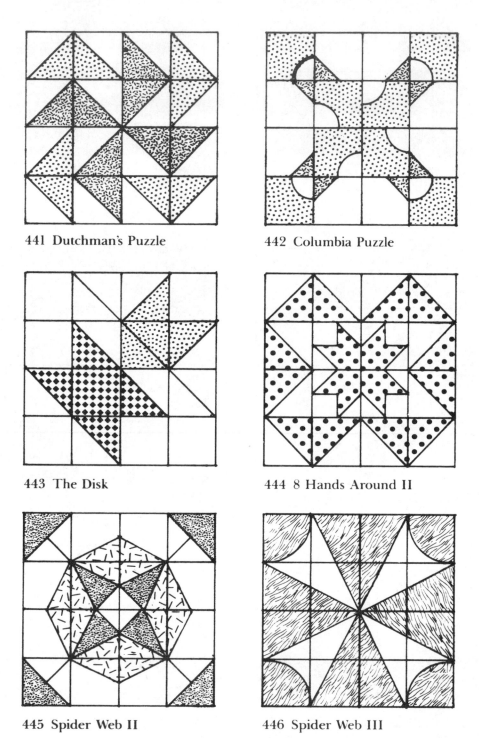

441 Dutchman's Puzzle

442 Columbia Puzzle

443 The Disk

444 8 Hands Around II

445 Spider Web II

446 Spider Web III

447 Whirlwind

448 Fancy Stripe

449 Broken Dishes II

450 Four Points

451 Buzzard's Roost

452 Peace & Plenty

453 Broken Dishes III

454 Louisiana

455 Year's Favorite

456 Swastika I

457 Broken Dishes IV

458 Yankee Puzzle

459 Basket II

460 Bread Basket

461 Flower Pot II

462 Tulip Basket

463 Bouquet

464 Tea Basket

101

465 Mayflower

466 Secret Drawer

467 Double-Z I

468 Hourglass III

469 Double-Z II

470 Colorado Block

471 Centennial II

472 Square & Star

473 Boy's Nonsense

474 Square & Compass

475 Storm at Sea

476 Windblown Square

477 Mill & Star

478 Flying Dutchman II

479 Chinese Puzzle

480 Wild Waves

481 Turkey Giblets

482 Pinwheel II

483 Bachelor's Puzzle I

484 End of Day

485 Windmill II

486 Arkansas Traveller II

487 Pinwheel III

488 Whirlpool

489 V-Block I

490 V-Block II

491 Ribbon Block

492 Ribbons II

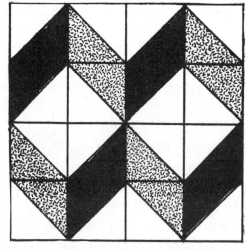

493 Grandma's Red & White

494 Maltese Cross

495 Grandmother's Own III

496 Swastika II

497 Cotton Reels

498 Brave World

499 Waste Not

500 Hither & Yon

501 Hovering Birds

502 Mother's Dream II

503 Flying-X

504 Windflower

505 Windmill III

506 Yankee Charm

507 Flying Bats

508 Arrow Star

509 Crown of Thorns

510 Constellation

511 Dogtooth Violet

512 Flying Fish

513 Dutch Windmill

514 Double Pinwheel III

515 Whirligig I

516 Whirligig II

517 July 4th

518 Windmill IV

519 Cross Within Cross

520 Magic Circle

521 Posy Patch

522 Annamac's Star

523 Morning Star II

524 Star & Cone

525 Ladies Wreath II

526 Pinwheel IV

527 Cross on Cross

528 Old Windmill

529 Children of Israel

530 Ozark Trail

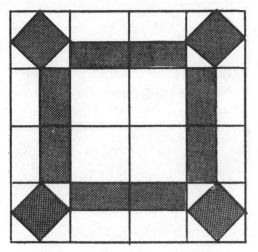

531 Johnnie Around the Corner

532 Tulip Lady Fingers II

533 Puss in the Corner III

534 Triangles & Stripe

535 I Do

536 Formal Garden II

537 Star & Crown

538 Wheel of Fortune I

539 Drucilla's Delight

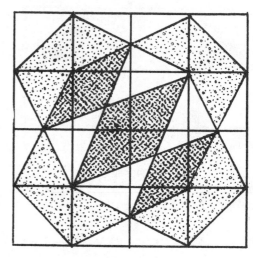

540 Dove in the Window

541 Beautiful Star

542 North Star

114

543 Granny's Choice

544 Bowtie

545 Broken Path

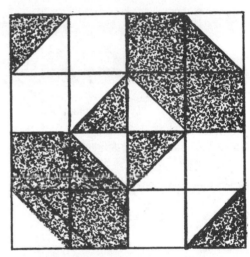

546 Robbing Peter to Pay Paul II

547 Sunshiny Day

548 Starry Path

549 Calico Bouquet

550 Tea Leaf

551 Little Lost Sailboat

552 Crazy Quilt Flower

553 Ship

554 Crazy Quilt

555 Log Cabin II

556 Tall Pine Tree

557 Rainbow Block

558 Butterfly II

559 Indian Hatchet I

560 Tulip II

561 4-Patch Chain

562 Hull's Victory

563 Blockade

564 Friendship

565 Friday the 13th

566 Rail Fence IV

567 Beacon Lights

568 Noon & Light

569 Laurel Wreath

570 Royal Star

571 Country Path

572 Ft. Sumter

573 Tea Rose

574 Crazy Ann I

575 Interlocking Squares

576 Interwoven Puzzle

577 White House Steps

578 Three Crosses

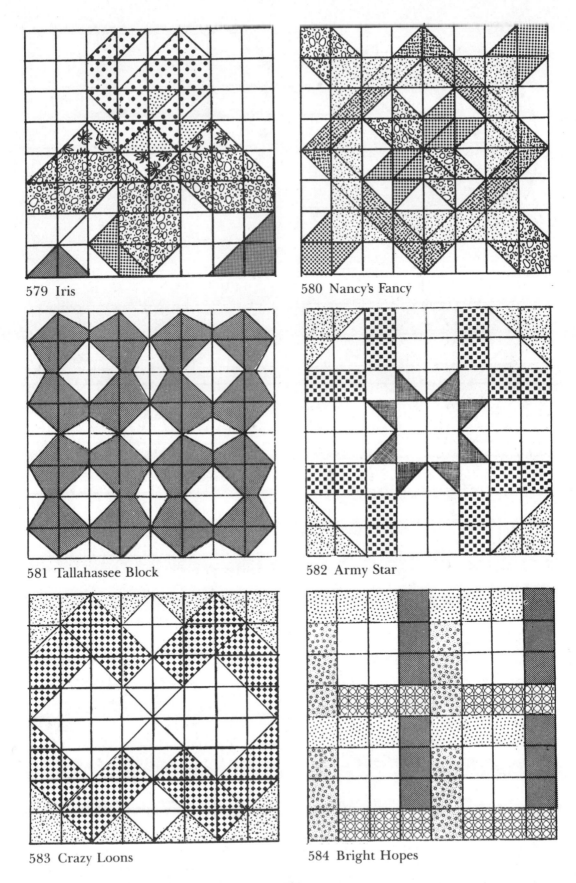

579 Iris

580 Nancy's Fancy

581 Tallahassee Block

582 Army Star

583 Crazy Loons

584 Bright Hopes

585 Flower Basket II

586 Arizona Star

587 Shaded Trail

588 Tree of Temptation

589 Tree of Life I

590 Nosegay II

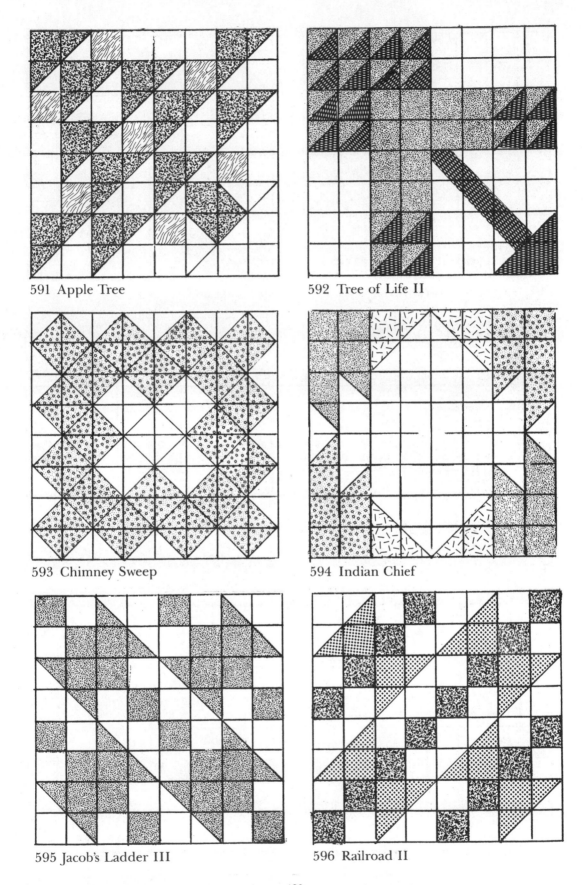

591 Apple Tree

592 Tree of Life II

593 Chimney Sweep

594 Indian Chief

595 Jacob's Ladder III

596 Railroad II

597 Georgetown Circles

598 Railroad Crossing I

599 Providence Block I

600 Eddystone Light

601 Barrister's Block

602 Kansas Troubles

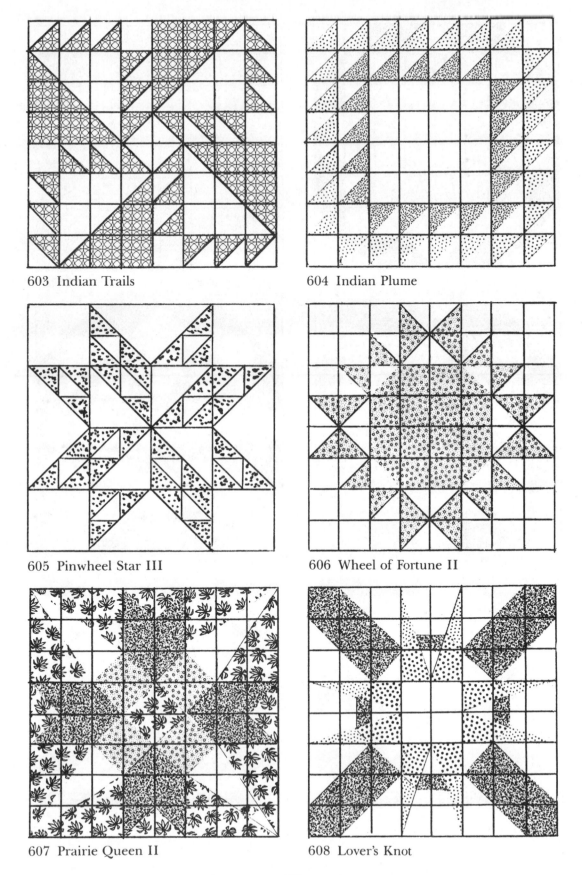

603 Indian Trails

604 Indian Plume

605 Pinwheel Star III

606 Wheel of Fortune II

607 Prairie Queen II

608 Lover's Knot

609 Diamond Star

610 Farmer's Fields

611 Rolling Star I

612 Star & Chains

613 Alaska

614 Harbor View

615 Cross & Square

616 West Virginia

617 Jewel Box

618 Pride of Ohio

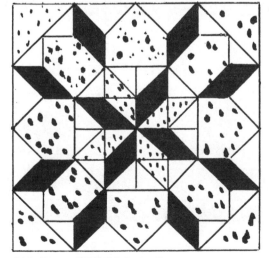

619 Star of Bethlehem I

620 Waterwheel

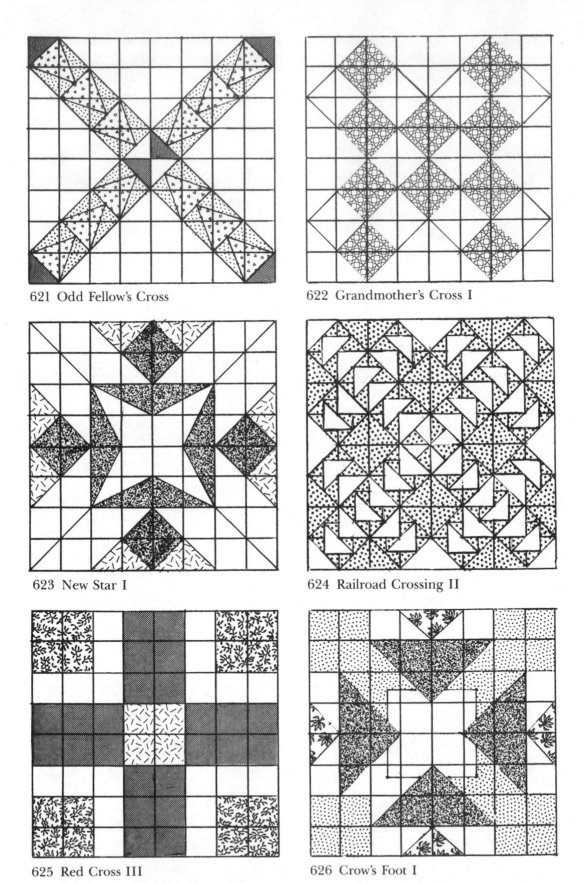

621 Odd Fellow's Cross

622 Grandmother's Cross I

623 New Star I

624 Railroad Crossing II

625 Red Cross III

626 Crow's Foot I

627 Little Giant

628 Springfield

629 Irish Chain

630 Flying Clouds I

631 Crow's Foot II

632 Delectable Mountains

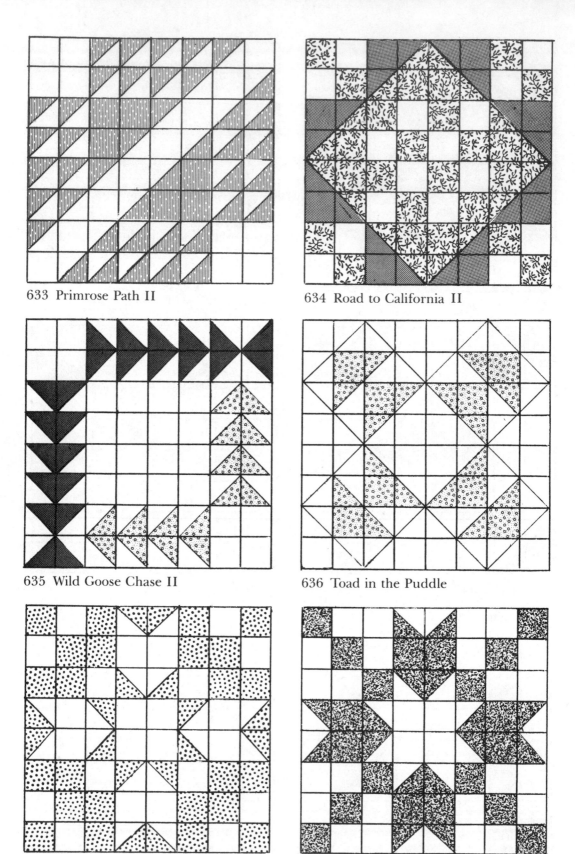

633 Primrose Path II

634 Road to California II

635 Wild Goose Chase II

636 Toad in the Puddle

637 Blackford's Beauty

638 Stepping Stones

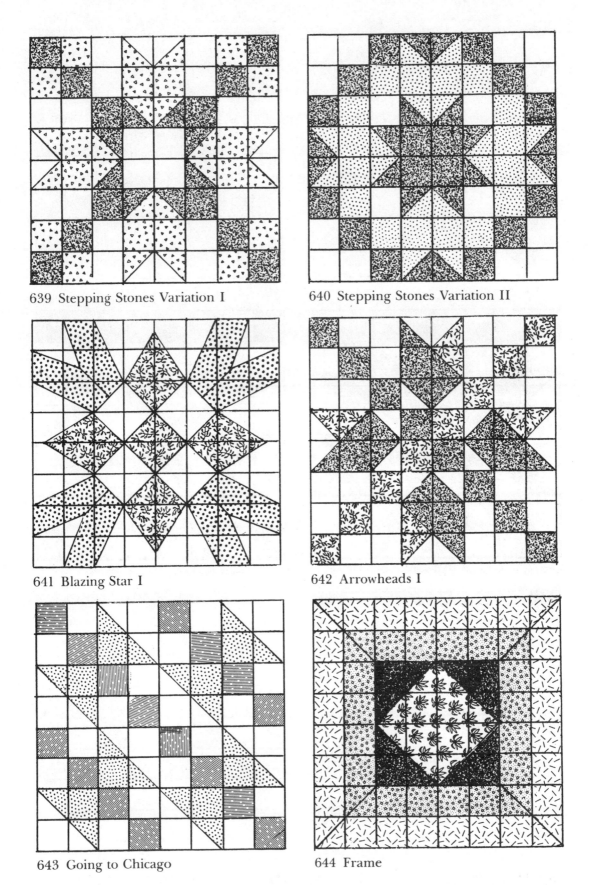

639 Stepping Stones Variation I

640 Stepping Stones Variation II

641 Blazing Star I

642 Arrowheads I

643 Going to Chicago

644 Frame

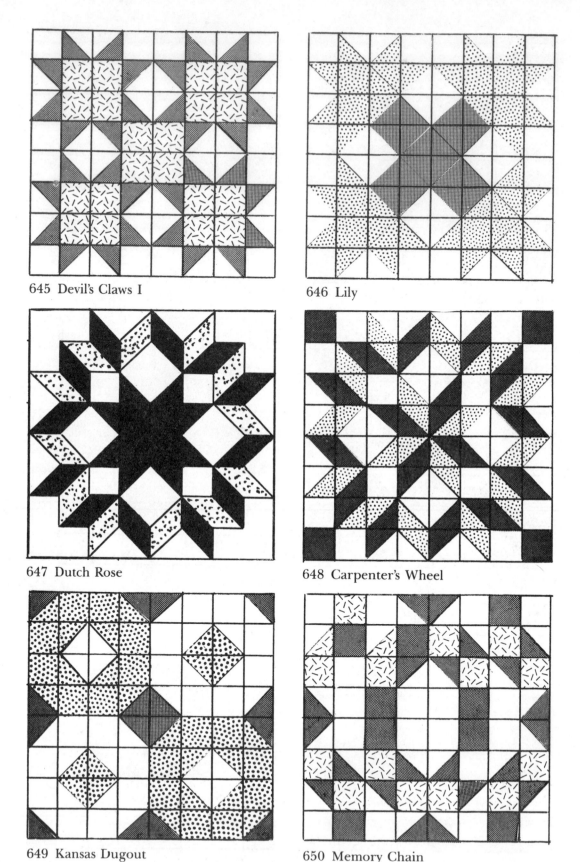

645 Devil's Claws I

646 Lily

647 Dutch Rose

648 Carpenter's Wheel

649 Kansas Dugout

650 Memory Chain

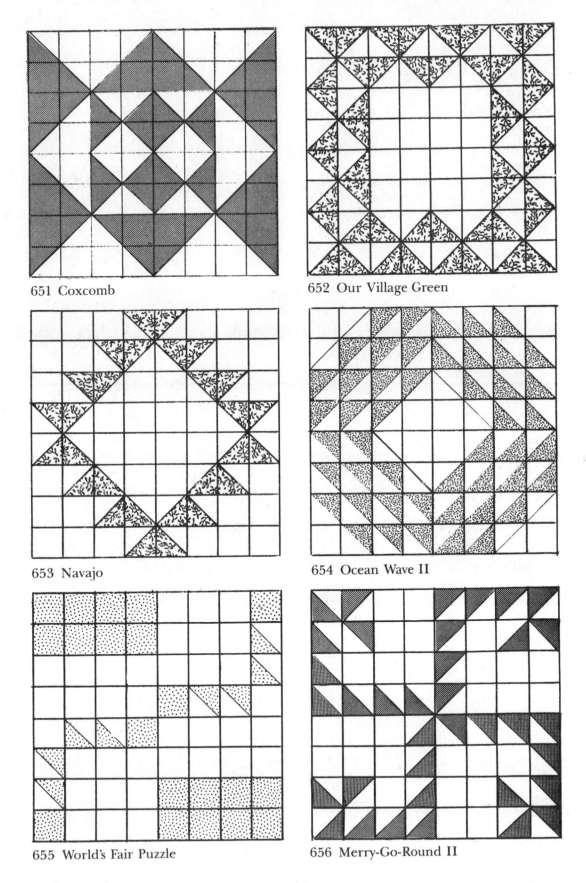

651 Coxcomb

652 Our Village Green

653 Navajo

654 Ocean Wave II

655 World's Fair Puzzle

656 Merry-Go-Round II

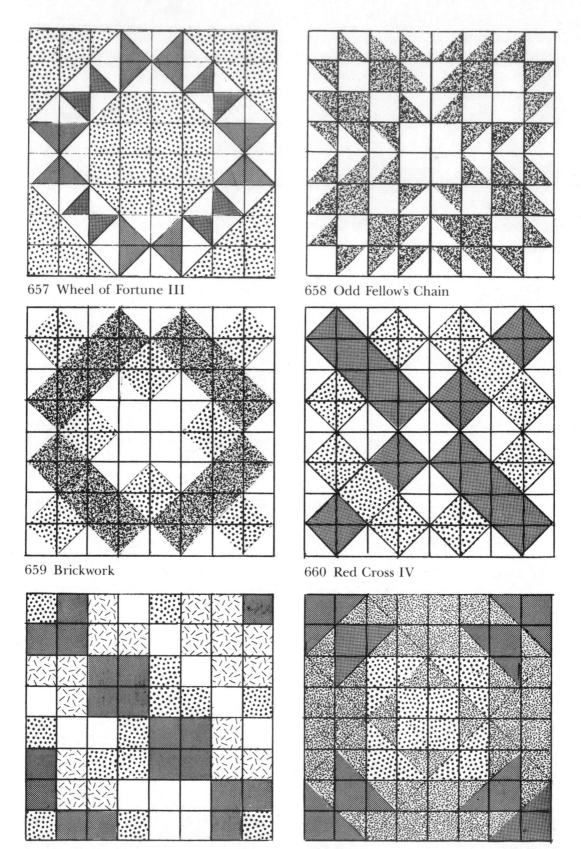

657 Wheel of Fortune III

658 Odd Fellow's Chain

659 Brickwork

660 Red Cross IV

661 Steps to Glory

662 Rambler

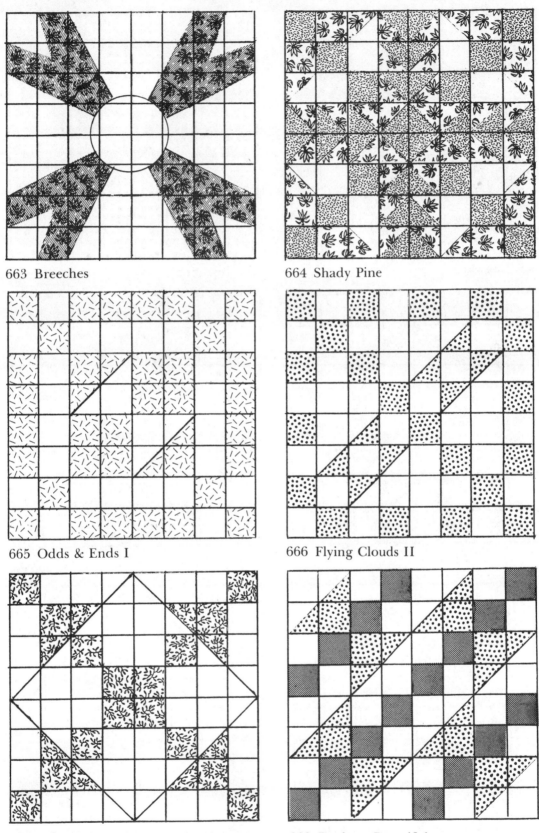

663 Breeches

664 Shady Pine

665 Odds & Ends I

666 Flying Clouds II

667 Fanny's Favorite

668 Buckeye Beautiful

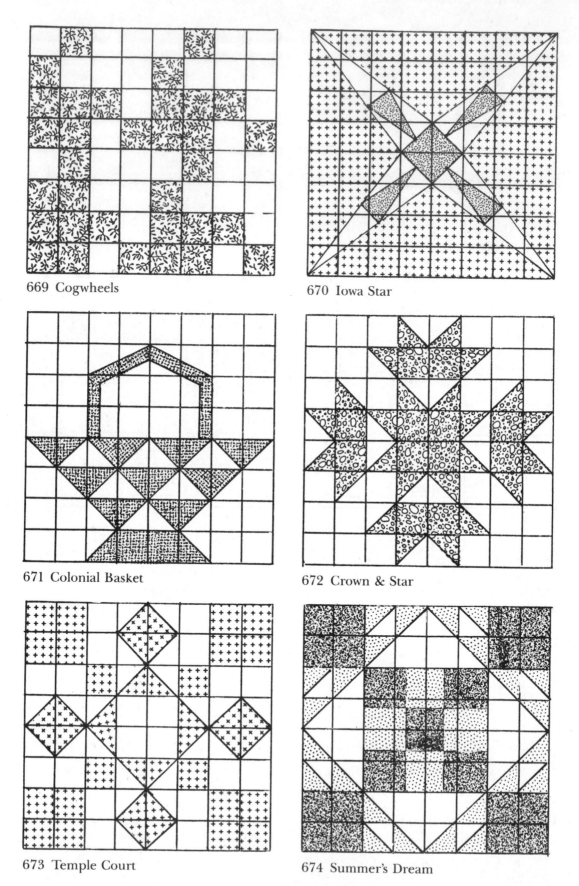

669 Cogwheels

670 Iowa Star

671 Colonial Basket

672 Crown & Star

673 Temple Court

674 Summer's Dream

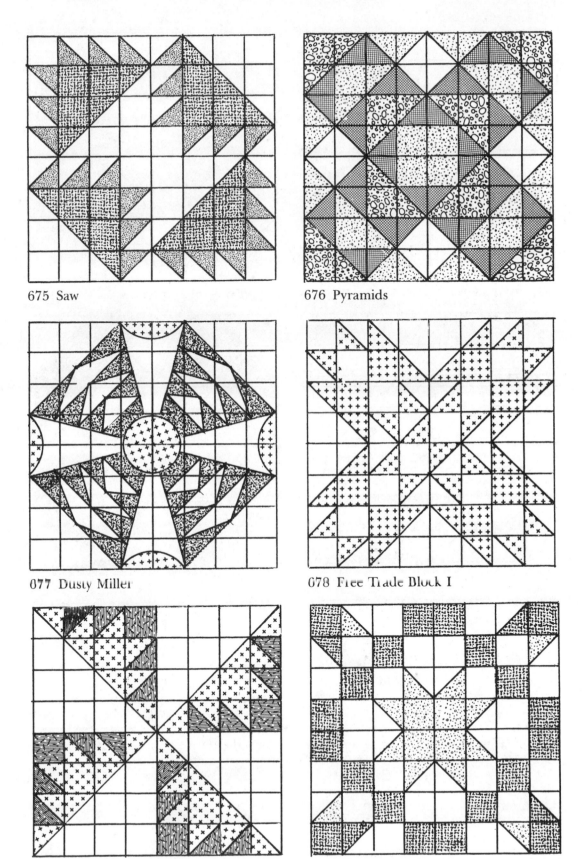

675 Saw

676 Pyramids

677 Dusty Miller

678 Free Trade Block I

679 Grand Right & Left

680 Kaleidoscope II

681 Sunny Lanes

682 Postage Stamp Basket

683 Square Deal

684 Cupid's Arrowpoint

685 Lost Children

686 Coffin Star

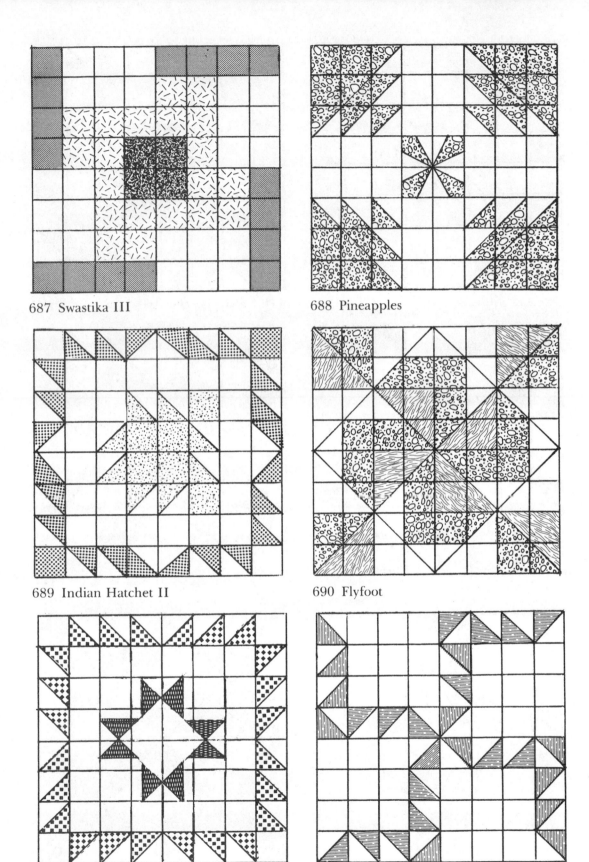

687 Swastika III

688 Pineapples

689 Indian Hatchet II

690 Flyfoot

691 Blindman's Fancy

692 Century

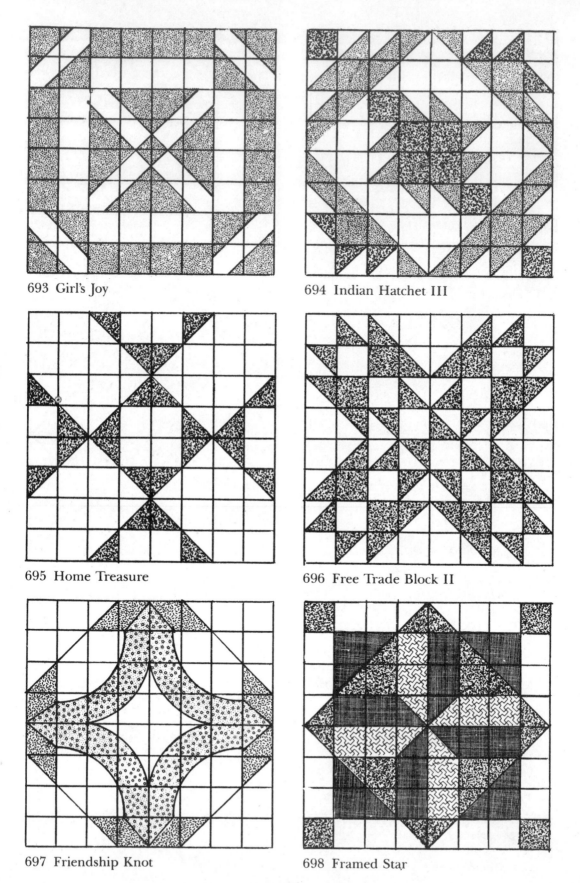

693 Girl's Joy

694 Indian Hatchet III

695 Home Treasure

696 Free Trade Block II

697 Friendship Knot

698 Framed Star

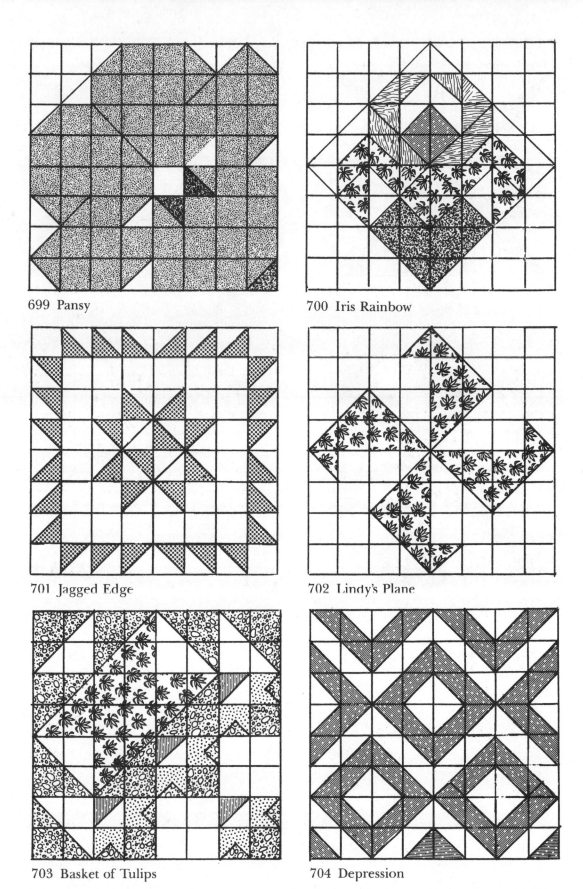

699 Pansy

700 Iris Rainbow

701 Jagged Edge

702 Lindy's Plane

703 Basket of Tulips

704 Depression

705 Thorny Thicket

706 Sailboat

707 Chuck-a-Luck

708 Hanging Basket

Five-Patch Designs

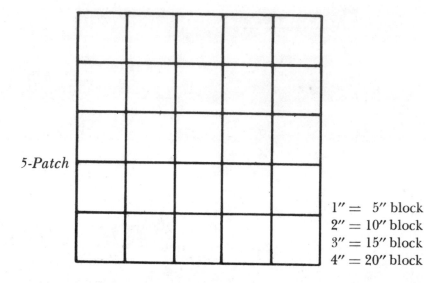

5-Patch

1″ = 5″ block
2″ = 10″ block
3″ = 15″ block
4″ = 20″ block

5-Patch—Each Square Divided in Half

1″ = 10″ block
2″ = 20″ block

There are also a few 5-patch designs, divided into thirds, making a total of 15 squares across.

709 Children's Delight

710 5-Patch

711 Plaid I

712 Bat Wing

713 Broken Arrows I

714 Broken Arrows II

715 Pigeon Toes

716 Mare's Nest

717 Flying Square

718 Domino

719 Ladies' Delight

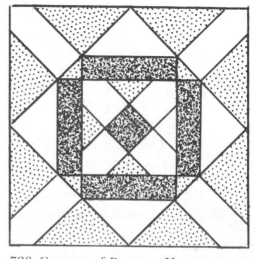

720 Century of Progress II

721 Star & Cross

722 Blocks in a Box

723 Easy Do

724 Dutch Mill

725 Captain's Wheel

726 Handy Andy III

727 Fool's Square

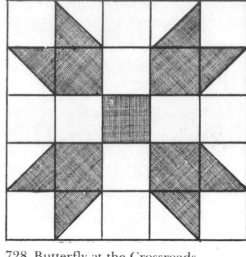

728 Butterfly at the Crossroads

729 Sister's Choice

730 E-Z Quilt

731 Providence Block II

732 Four & Star

733 Farmer's Daughter

734 Jack in the Box

735 Follow the Leader

736 Crazy Ann II

737 Clown

738 Honey's Choice

739 Leap Frog

740 Widower's Choice

741 Bachelor's Puzzle II

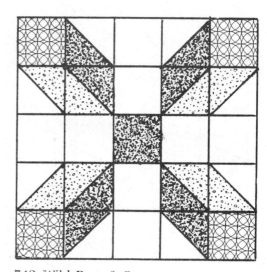

742 Wild Rose & Square

743 Rolling Star II

744 Jack's Blocks

745 Double Sawtooth II

746 Lady of the Lake II

747 Flying Geese

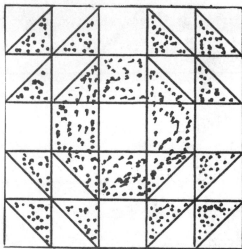

748 Single Wedding Ring II

749 Square & a Half

750 Handy Andy III

751 Greek Cross II

752 King's Crown II

753 Star of Hope

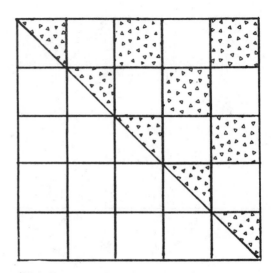

754 Steps to the Altar III

755 Pine Tree III

756 Christmas Tree

152

757 King David's Crown

758 Album III

759 Red Cross V

760 Duck & Ducklings I

761 Domino Square

762 Ombre

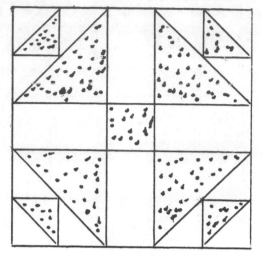

763 Duck & Ducklings II

764 Bird's Nest

765 David & Goliath

766 Bull's Eye

767 Doe & Darts

768 Cross & Crown

769 Fruit Basket

770 Southern Pine

771 Grape Basket

772 Flower Basket

773 Flower Pot III

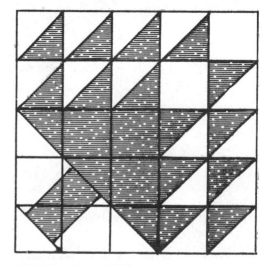

774 Pine Tree IV

155

775 Devil's Claws II

776 Four-Leaf Clover

777 Philadelphia Pavement

778 Oregon

779 Queen Charlotte's Crown

780 Propeller

781 Wedding Rings

782 Mrs. Keller's 9-Patch

783 New Star II

784 Cross & Star

785 Hope of Hartford

786 Washington Puzzle

787 Garden of Eden

788 Grandmother's Cross

789 Swallows

790 Turkey Tracks III

791 Pieced Tulip

792 Eagle

793 Cluster of Stars

794 Golden Royalty

795 Stylized Flower

796 Kicks

797 Crazy House

798 Disney Fantasy

799 Churn Dash

800 Double Wrench

801 Pinwheel Square

802 Grandmother's Choice I

803 Grandmother's Choice II

804 Alaska Homestead

805 Minnesota

806 Cousteau's Calypso

807 St. Louis Block

808 Georgia

809 Idaho

810 Joseph's Coat II

811 Cakestand

812 Z-Cross

813 Tent of Armageddon

814 Wishing Ring

815 Double Irish Chain

816 Shooting Star III

817 Japanese Poppy

818 Milky Way I

819 Dutch Waterways

820 Old Fashioned Daisy

821 Carpenter's Square

822 Pine Tree V

823 Linton

824 Mexican Cross

825 Milky Way II

826 Little Beech Tree

827 Tree of Paradise

828 Autumn Leaves

829 Grape Vine

830 Grandmother's Pinwheel

831 Indian Squares

832 Old Maid's Ramble

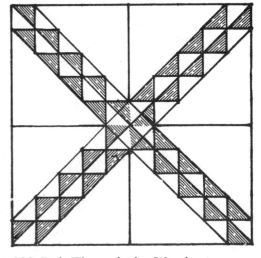

833 Path Through the Woods

Hexagrams, Circles, Diamonds, and Stars

On a large sheet of paper draw a square the final size of the block. Rule it into the same number of squares as shown in the pattern. Draw in the lines in each square.

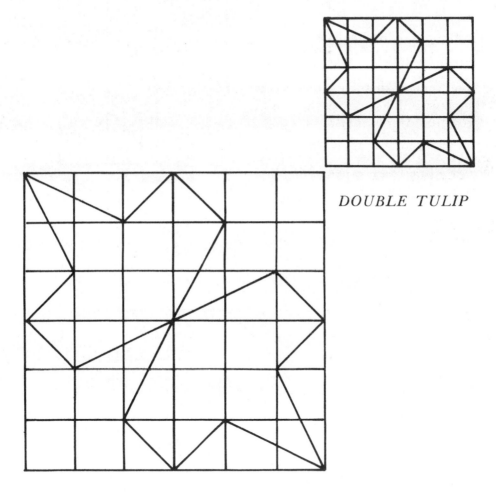

DOUBLE TULIP

CIRCLES

Circles can be drawn by using plates, saucers, cups, pan lids, and so forth, in the appropriate size. This seems a rather haphazard method, but I've never found the string and pencil method satisfactory, and I've yet to find a compass that will draw an 18″ circle.

The pattern pieces for designs such as Tobacco Leaf are made by laying the circle template's edge at the corner of the square. Position it so that it crosses the corner of the center square. Trace around the template. Repeat for the other edge of the elliptical shape.

Trace octagon onto full-size block. Lay a ruler along edges and enlarge to proper size.

Draw in guidelines as shown.

Find length of this line to center.

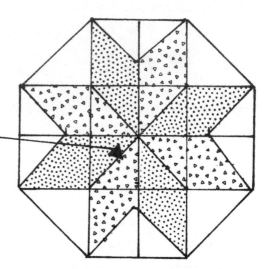

From center, measure along center lines outward the same distance as the arrow line. Mark with a dot.

Draw a line from corner to dot. Your diamond is complete.

There are plastic templates available for both 45° and 60° diamond shapes, as well as for hexagons, but it's always nice to be able to draft the shape to fit your block exactly.

834 Triple Irish Chain

835 Lily of the Field

836 Cathedral Window

837 Pine Burr I

838 Odd Star

839 Kite's Tail

840 Pine Burr II

841 Church Steps

842 Zig Zag

843 Solomon's Temple

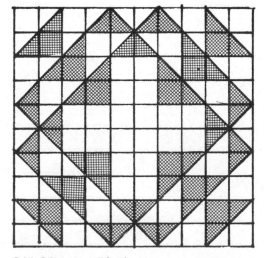

844 Memory Block

170

6-POINT STAR

The 6-point star is based on a hexagon.

Enlarge the hexagon by laying a ruler along each edge and marking it up until it is the desired size for the block.

Draw in the guidelines as shown, beginning with the lines touching the outer edges, and ending with the center lines.

846 Wedding Tile

845 Merry-Go-Round III

847 Jack's Chain

848 Whirligig III

849 Spider Web IV

850 Eisenhower Star

851 Tea Box

852 Columbia

853 Castle Wall

854 Rising Sun

855 Old Glory

856 Kentucky

857 Octagon

858 Robbing Peter to Pay Paul III

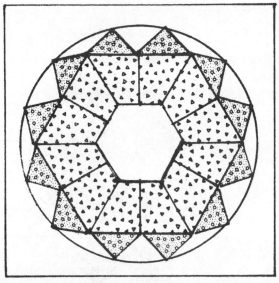

859 Queen of the May

860 Liberty Star

861 Virginia Star

862 Tennessee Star

175

863 Peony I

864 Flying Swallows

865 King's Crown III

866 Missouri

867 Chained Star

868 Star of LeMoyne

869 Aurora Borealis

870 Aunt Martha's Rose

871 Orange Peel II

872 Skyscraper

873 Tumbling Hexagons I

874 Ozark Diamonds

875 Colorado Star

876 Snow Crystal

877 Jewel II

878 Silver & Gold

879 Pinwheel Star

880 · Lucinda's Star

881 Flying Saucer

882 Block Puzzle I

883 Old Staffordshire

884 8 Diamonds & a Star

885 Meadow Flower

886 Kaleidoscope III

887 Hexagon Beauty

888 Madison Block

889 Block Puzzle II

890 Star of Bethlehem II

891 Hexagon Star

892 Stop Sign

893 Interlocked Star

894 Wonder of Egypt

895 Diamond & Star

896 Cosmos

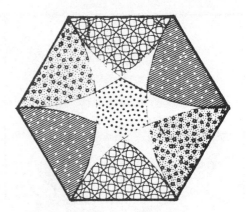

897 Star of the Mountains

898 Tumbling Hexagons II

899 Arrowheads II

900 Spider Web V

901 Mary's Fan

902 Four O'clock

903 Circle within Circle

904 Electric Fan

905 Texas Tulip

906 Air Ship Propeller

907 Alabama Beauty

908 Homemaker

909 Indiana

910 Country Crossroads

911 Caesar's Crown

912 Crossroads

913 Fair Play

914 Nocturne

915 Josephine Knot

916 Hidden Flower

917 Butterfly III

918 Turtle

919 Queen's Crown I

920 Queen's Crown II

921 Pullman Puzzle I

922 Queen's Pride

923 Compass I

924 Old Maid Combination

925 Millwheel

926 Compass II

927 Shell

928 Utah

929 Old Missouri

930 Ohio Beauty

931 Grandmother's Fan I

932 Flo's Fan

933 Grandmother's Fan II

934 Fan

935 Patchwork Fan

936 Milady's Fan

937 Snake in the Hollow

938 Dresden Plate

939 Circle of Life

940 Grandmother's Choice IV

941 Mushrooms

942 Moon & Stars

943 Arkansas II

944 Rainbow Star

945 Nevada

946 Fancy Dresden Plate

947 Ferris Wheel

948 Odds & Ends II

949 Baseball

950 Circle Cross

951 Bay Leaf

952 Orange Peel II

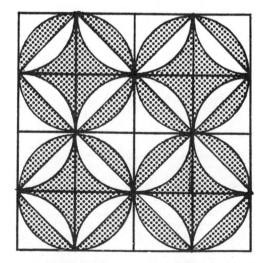

953 Robbing Peter to Pay Paul IV

954 Boston Puzzle I

955 Savannah Star

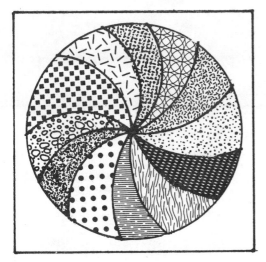

956 Wheel of Fortune IV

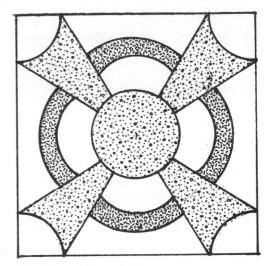

957 Sun, Moon & Stars

958 Tobacco Leaf

959 Trenton Quilt Block

960 Drunkard's Path

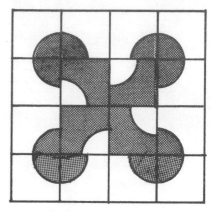

961 Wonder of the World

962 Falling Timbers

963 Vine of Friendship

964 Dove I

965 Fool's Puzzle I

966 Chain Links

967 Love Ring

968 Polka Dot

969 Snowball II

970 Grandmother's Favorite

971 Snowball III

972 Unnamed

973 Steeplechase

974 Snowball Wreath

975 Pullman Puzzle

976 Robbing Peter to Pay Paul V

977 Winding Ways

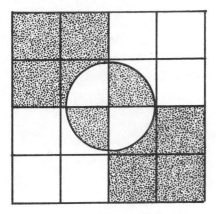

978 Robbing Peter to Pay Paul VI

979 Around the World

980 Drunkard's Path Variation

981 Fool's Puzzle II

982 Millwheel II

983 Boston Puzzle II

Seven-Patch
Designs

984 Hobby Horse

985 Walls of Jericho

986 Dove II

987 Red Cross VI

988 Rosebud III

989 City Square

990 Country Roads

991 Prickly Pear

992 Bear's Paw

993 Bear's Tracks

994 Stonemason's Puzzle

995 Lincoln's Platform

996 Autumn Leaf

997 Peony II

998 Hens & Chickens

999 9-Patch VI

1000 Hemstitch

1001 Blazing Star II

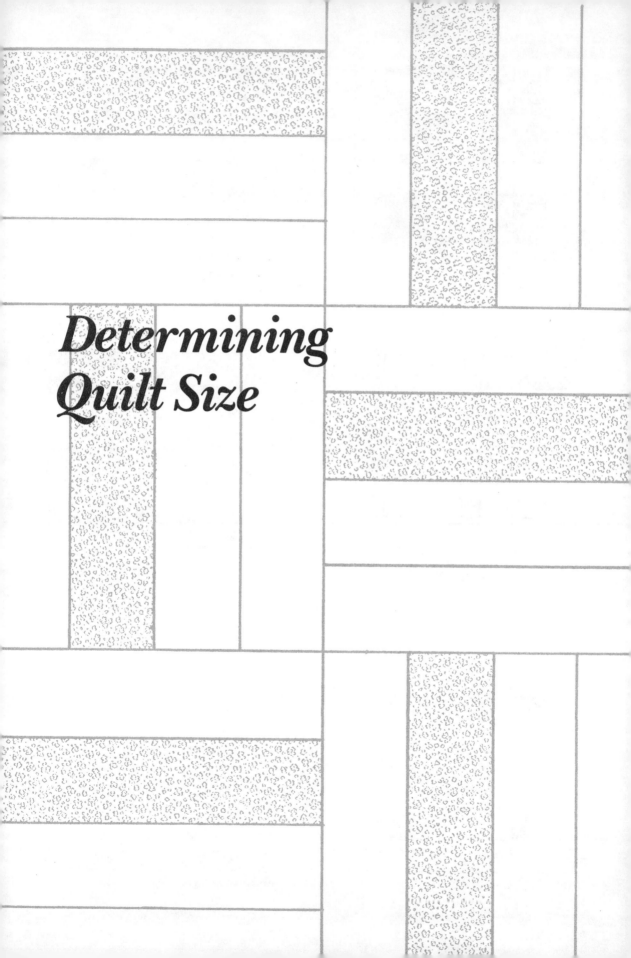

Determining
Quilt Size

To determine quilt size, several factors must be taken into account. Mattress size is your first consideration. Then, do you want the quilt to fall to the floor as a bedspread, with tuck-in for the pillows, or just as a cover for the mattress? Does the style of the bed present limitations? I have an antique bed with sideboards measuring 14″ deep. I don't want the quilt to fall below the sideboards, so I am limited in the amount of overhang. A throw for the couch would be smaller, as would a baby quilt.

As a general guideline, mattress sizes are as follows:

King	72″ × 84″
Queen	60″ × 80″
Double	54″ × 75″
Twin	39″ × 75″
Cot	30″ × 75″
Crib	27″ × 50″

It's a good idea to go ahead and measure your mattress, especially if it suffers from middle-age spread. Measure from side-to-side to obtain width, and from top-to-bottom for length.

For a double-size bed, my calculations would be as follows:

Mattress size:	54″ wide × 75″ long
Allowance for pillows:	18″
Overhang at foot:	12″
Overhang on each side:	
12″ × 2 =	24″
	78″ wide × 105″ long

The next example is for a modern bed, with a double-size mattress. Mattress and box springs have a depth of 14″ and the quilt will not cover the pillows:

Mattress size:	54″ wide × 75″ long
Overhang at foot:	14″
Overhang on each side:	
14″ × 2 =	28″
	82″ wide × 89″ long

Once you've decided how large you want the quilt it's time to determine what size block you will use. You should be flexible in this area, because block size and finished quilt size usually will not come out even. The following charts illustrate the problems that arise in arriving at an approximate quilt size of 78″ × 106″:

Block Size	Blocks Across	Blocks Down	Total Blocks Needed
8″	9 = 72″ 6″ border	13 = 104″ 2″ border	117
9″	8 = 72″ 6″ border	11 = 99″ 7″ border	88
10″	7 = 70″ 8″ border	10 = 100″ 6″ border	70
12″	6 = 72″ 6″ border	8 = 96″ 10″ border	48
14″	5 = 70″ 8″ border	7 = 98″ 8″ border	35
15″	5 = 75″ 3″ border	7 = 105″ 1″ border	35

or

Block Size	Blocks Across	Blocks Down	Total Blocks Needed
15″	4 = 60″ 18″ border	6 = 90″ 16″ border	24
16″	4 = 64″ 14″ border	6 = 96″ 10″ border	24
18″	4 = 72″ 6″ border	5 = 90″ 16″ border	20

As you can see, only the 14″ block size will come out evenly. If you are using a 7-patch pattern, you're in good shape and can proceed full steam ahead. However, if using any of the others, when scaling your pattern to the 14″ size, you will have to work with fractions. I avoid this at all costs and would make adjustments in the finished size.

If you decide to use a 12″ block, you can either increase the side borders to equal 10″ or cut down the end border to measure 6″. This is much simpler than working with fractions to scale the block to the 14″ size.

The above examples are for use when the patchwork is an overall design. If you wish, you can piece only the portion that will cover the mattress top and fill in the sides with borders to show off your fancy quilting stitches.

Setting the quilt with lattice strips is a very popular method. In fact, in the above examples it would be easier to set the 18″ block this way, rather than to try to adjust the borders to allow for 10″. The following chart shows the calculations and adjustments needed when using lattice strips. The quilt size is 78″ x 106″ and border and lattice strips are figured to be the same width.

Block Size	Blocks Across	Blocks Down	Total Blocks Needed
8″	8 = 64″ 9 2″ strips = 18″ Finished Size: 82″ × 102″	10 = 80″ 11 2″ strips = 22″	80
9″	7 = 63″ 8 2″ strips = 16″ Finished Size: 79″ × 101″	9 = 81″ 10 2″ strips = 20″	63
10″	6 = 60″ 7 3″ strips = 21″ Finished Size: 81″ × 107″	8 = 80″ 9 3″ strips = 27″	48
12″	5 = 60″ 6 3″ strips = 18″ Finished Size: 78″ × 108″	7 = 84″ 8 3″ strips = 24″	35
14″	4 = 56″ 5 3″ strips = 15″ Finished Size: 71″ × 105″ (This size may be better if set solid.)	6 = 84″ 7 3″ strips = 21″	24
15″	4 = 60″ 5 3″ strips = 15″ Finished Size: 75″ × 94″ *If the lattice strips are made 4″ wide:* 5 4″ strips = 20″ Finished Size: 80″ × 99″	5 = 75″ 6 3″ strips = 18″ 6 4″ strips = 24″	20
16″	4 = 64″ 5 4″ strips = 20″ Finished Size: 84″ × 104″	5 = 80″ 6 4″ strips = 24″	20
18″	3 = 54″ 4 4″ strips = 16″ Finished Size: 70″ × 92″	4 = 72″ 5 4″ strips = 20″	

The lattice strips could be increased to 5″ or 6″ in width.

Blocks set on the diagonal must be multiplied by 1.42 to determine the finished size of the quilt. The following shows the width of the blocks and rounds it off to the nearest ½.

$$8'' \text{ block} = 11.36 \text{ or } 11\frac{1}{2}''$$
$$9'' \text{ block} = 12.78 \text{ or } 13''$$
$$10'' \text{ block} = 14.2 \text{ or } 14''$$
$$11'' \text{ block} = 15.62 \text{ or } 15\frac{1}{2}''$$
$$12'' \text{ block} = 17.04 \text{ or } 17''$$
$$13'' \text{ block} = 18.46 \text{ or } 18\frac{1}{2}''$$
$$14'' \text{ block} = 19.88 \text{ or } 20''$$
$$15'' \text{ block} = 21.3 \text{ or } 21\frac{1}{2}''$$
$$16'' \text{ block} = 22.72 \text{ or } 22\frac{1}{2}''$$
$$17'' \text{ block} = 24.14 \text{ or } 24''$$
$$18'' \text{ block} = 25.56 \text{ or } 25\frac{1}{2}''$$

The foregoing may seem like a lot of unnecessary math, but some familiarity with it will be helpful to you. Before you can figure the amount of fabric to buy, you must know how many blocks you need to complete the top. For a double bed, you can get some idea just by using the figures given here. Even if you have to figure it out, you'll only have to do it once since you're making quilts for the same size bed most of the time. I almost always use a 12" block, the quilt set solid with no border, so I automatically know I need 48 blocks.

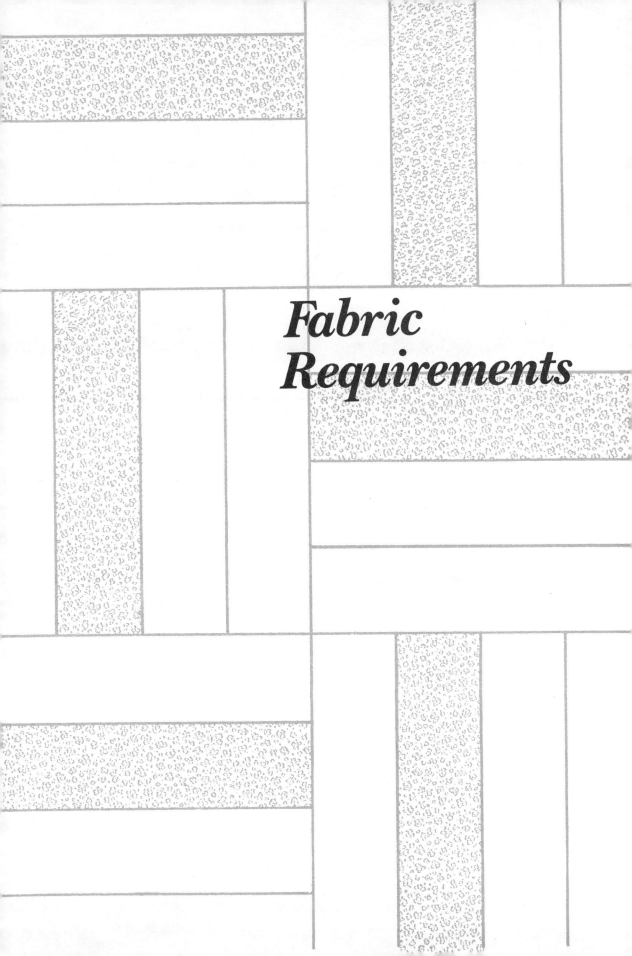

Fabric Requirements

Once you have determined how many blocks are needed for the quilt top you are ready to estimate how much fabric you need. I'll use the Friendship Star, p. 000, scaled to a 12″ block as an example.

Step 1: Determine total number of units per block.

   4 white squares, 1 colored square
   4 white triangles, 4 colored triangles

Step 2: Multiply by total number of blocks.

   $4 \times 48 = 192$ white squares
            192 colored triangles
            192 white triangles
             48 colored squares

Step 3: Add seam allowances to one of each of the units needed. Measure width and length of each of these units.

Step 4: Find the unit width on the accompanying chart. Go across to the second column to find how many units can be cut across the width of the fabric.

   4″ square plus $\frac{1}{2}$″ seam allowance = 5″ square
   9 units across fabric

Step 5: Find the unit length on the chart and follow it across to the third column to see how many units can be cut from the length of the fabric.

   4″ square plus $\frac{1}{2}$″ seam allowance = 5″ square
   7 units down fabric

Step 6: Multiply the number of units obtained in width by the number of units obtained in length to determine how many units can be cut from 1 yard of fabric.

   9 units across $\times$ 7 units down = 63 per yard

Step 7: Divide total number of units needed by number of units per yard to obtain total yardage required.

   192 divided by 63 = 3.04 yards
   Repeat for each unit of block.

Unit Size	Number of Units Across (45" fabric)	Number of Units Down (36" fabric)
1"	45	36
1½"	30	24
2"	22	18
2½"	18	14
3"	15	12
3½"	12	10
4"	11	9
4½"	10	8
5"	9	7
5½"	8	6
6"	7	6
6½"	6	5
7"	6	5
7½"	6	4
8"	5	4
8½"	5	4
9"	4	4

Quilting

Quilting is the finishing touch to your patchwork top. The main purpose of the quilting stitches is to hold the three layers of the quilt together, but it has evolved into a highly decorative design element. In fact, many excellent examples of tops that were quilted only are in museums around the country. For many, this is the most enjoyable part of making the quilt.

As I've already mentioned, I like designing the tops, and don't get that involved with the actual quilting. I do it all on the machine to get it over with. Surprisingly, even intricate feather patterns can be executed on the sewing machine, if you've taken the time to learn what your machine can do.

Fillers or Batts

The filler is the material that goes in the middle, between the top and the lining.

Cotton batts. A cotton material in batt form. It must be closely quilted, with no more than an inch between the quilting lines because the batt will shift and bunch up when washed. It gives a rather flat appearance to the finished quilting.

Bonded polyester batts. This is a polyester material which has been treated to hold the fibres together. It is easy to work with since the layers of the batt will not shred or tear, giving a smooth uniform surface. The finished quilt has a higher loft and the quilting stitches stand out in relief. It need not be quilted as closely as cotton batts; two to four inches is usually sufficient.

Unbonded batts. These batts give a very soft, fluffy appearance to the finished quilt. Like the bonded batts, they are easy to work with during the sewing step, but care must be taken when spreading the batt on the top since it will shred, leaving thick and thin spots. You will have to pull off pieces from the thick spots or along the edges to fill in the thin spots. It, too, can be quilted two to four inches apart.

Lining or Backing Fabrics

Your choice is unlimited as to what you use to back your quilt with; yard goods, sheets, flannel or lightweight blankets are all suitable. You can still occasionally pick up fabrics for under a dollar a yard when the fabric stores have sales. Sheets are frequently on sale at very reasonable prices and can be used both for the backing and as material for the top. If you're near an outlet store, fabrics can be purchased for about half of what you would pay at your ordinary retail store. And don't overlook flea markets and rummage sales. You won't often find good fabrics here, but now and then you may hit a bonanza.

Assembling the Quilt

Lay the top wrong-side-up on a large, flat surface. Spread the batting over the top and smooth it out.

Seam the backing fabric together to the width of the quilt top, plus 1″ or 2″ all around. This extra allowance is especially important when doing machine quilting. This extra margin of fabric allows for any shifting of the fabric as you sew.

Whole-top Quilting

Step one is to loosen the pressure on the presser foot. This helps cut down on the shifting and pushing of the fabric, which is the major problem in machine quilting.

Do not baste the layers of the quilt together. I place several large pins around the edges of the quilt to help hold it while I begin sewing. If you baste, the fabric tends to pile up on the basting stitches causing puckers and ripples. By cutting the backing fabric slightly larger, I can smooth the fabric in front of the presser foot, taking out all wrinkles as I sew.

A large table on which to sew is an absolute must. It helps keep the quilt flat, cutting down on the amount of shifting you will experience. Position your sewing machine at one end of the table so you can spread the quilt out.

Slide the edge of the quilt under the presser foot and roll it up to the center. The center section is the most difficult because so much fabric is rolled under the machine. As you move out towards the edges, it gets easier. Following the seam line from the center, stitch to the outer edge of the quilt, smoothing out the fabric as you go. Do two or three rows in this direction, then turn the quilt and go in the opposite direction. This alternating technique helps keep the quilt smooth and flat.

If your top is of a simple design that requires only straight-line stitching, you can start at one end of the quilt and work to the other end. In this case, the backing fabric should be longer on the end toward which you are sewing so that any shift in the fabric is covered by the backing when finished. Always start sewing at the same end.

By the Block

This is an easy way to quilt, either by hand or machine, because you are working with only one block at a time. For intricate designs this method is by far the best, since the block is easy to manipulate under the needle.

Cut the filler the size of the finished block, and the backing one inch larger than the block. Lay the three layers together and quilt in the design, being sure that you do not quilt beyond the seam line into the seam allowance.

To assemble the blocks. Turn back the seam allowance on the backing and push the filler out of the way. Lay the quilted blocks right sides together and stitch the seams, being sure you do not catch in the backing or filler. Continue adding blocks until the first row is complete, then repeat for each succeeding row. Join the rows in the same manner.

Finishing the back. Smooth the batting down and trim off any excess. It should meet in the middle of the seam. Smooth one side of the backing down. Turn under the seam allowance on the other seam and lay over the first one. Stitch with a slipstitch.

A really nice finish for the back is to place lattice strips over the seams and stitch in place.

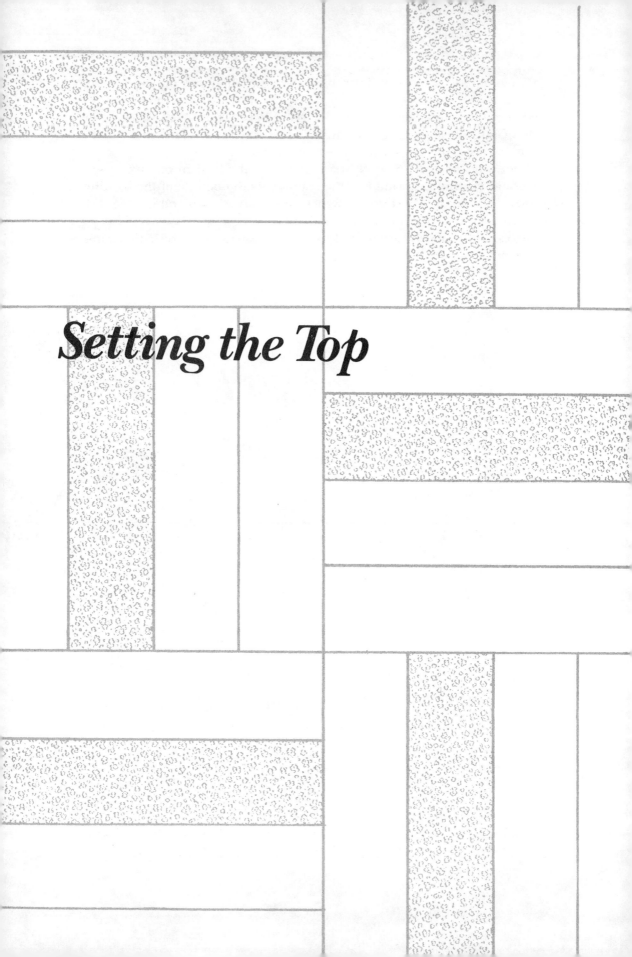

Setting the Top

The final step in assembling the quilt top is the setting. I find this to be the most exciting part of the entire quiltmaking process. Using the Ohio Star pattern, I've illustrated five different ways you can set the top, thereby giving you five different quilts.

The simplest method is to alternate plain and pieced blocks. With this setting you only have to piece half as many blocks, and it also provides more space for decorative quilting.

One of the most popular methods is to set the blocks solid. This setting gives an overall design, but many times you will be surprised. Secondary designs stand out only after the blocks have been assembled. The Wind-blown Square pattern is designed to be set with alternate white blocks, but I decided to set it solid. As illustrated, the basic design is lost and a pattern of pinwheels emerges.

The use of lattice strips to separate the blocks is another popular setting method, especially if the pattern has been executed in scrap fabrics. The lattice strips pull the design together into a coherent whole. And again, you don't need to piece as many blocks because the lattice strips add to the size of the quilt with little additional work.

Many blocks are designed to be set on the diagonal, but you should also try setting some of your favorite patterns diagonally. You may be pleasantly surprised by a stunning new quilt pattern.

Lattice strips are also effective on a diagonally set quilt. They can either blend in by being the same color as the background blocks or you can set the design off by using color in the strips. The long lines of solid color enhance and accentuate a diagonal design.

Color is the only important thing to consider when designing a quilt top. Color creates the design and whatever impact each design element has. It creates the tone and mood of the quilt. A design executed in browns, beiges and oranges will have a masculine feel, while the same design executed in pastels will be feminine in mood.

If you're new to quilting, don't let color frighten you. You can start by using the colors suggested in the pattern you're making. Or use colors that you like and use every day. When you shop for fabric, lay different colors together, then stand back and see what the effect of the combination is. Keep in mind that from a distance the design of the fabric doesn't show, only the color.

It's fun to experiment. All you need is some graph paper and colored markers. Draw the design on the graph paper and try out your ideas. If you have several you want to try, it would probably be easier to have some photocopies run of the design, so that you don't have to keep drawing it over and over.

The two Ohio Star variations came about using this method. The blue design is merely a change in color placement. The second one is achieved in the same manner, but the overall design doesn't come out until four blocks are set together. Lattice strips join each four-block unit.

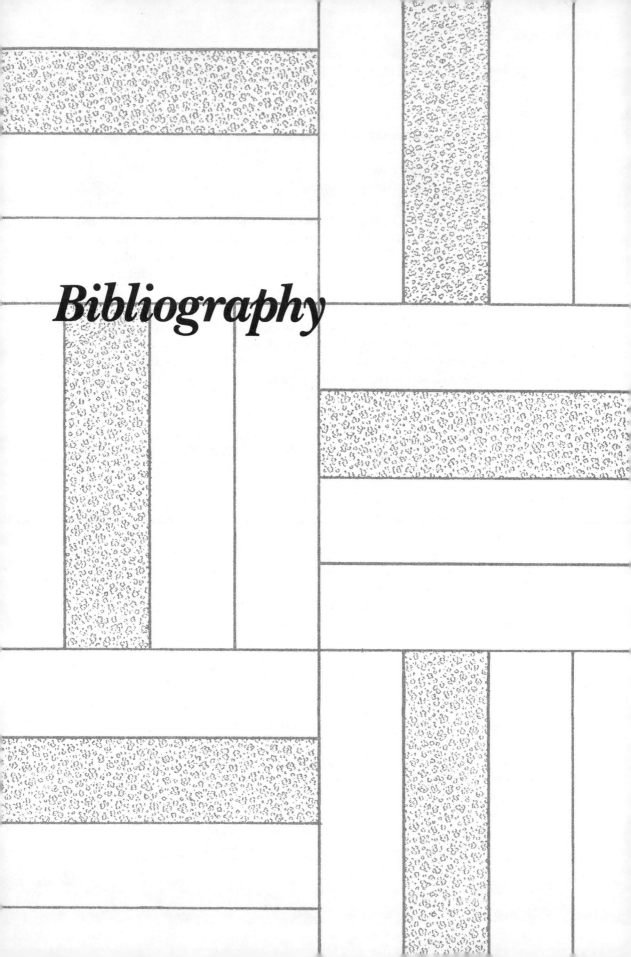

Bibliography

Bishop, Robert, *New Discoveries in American Quilts*. New York: E. P. Dutton & Company, 1975

Gutcheon, Beth, *The Perfect Patchwork Primer*. New York: Penguin Books, 1974

Hall, Carrie A. and Kretsinger, Rose G., *The Romance of the Patchwork Quilt in America*. New York: Bonanza Books, 1935

Hechtlinger, Adelaide, *American Quilts, Quilting and Patchwork*. Harrisburg, Pa.: Stackpole Books, 1974

Hinson, Dorothy A., *A Quilter's Companion*. New York: Arco Publishing Company, 1973

Holstein, Jonathan, *The Pieced Quilt, and American Design Tradition*. New York: New York Graphic Society, 1975

Ickis, Marguerite, *The Standard Book of Quilt Making and Collecting*. New York: Dover Publications, 1949

Khin, Yvonne M., *The Collectors Dictionary of Quilt Names and Patterns*. Washington, D.C.: Acropolis Books, 1980

Lithgow, Marilyn, *Quiltmaking & Quiltmakers*. New York: Funk & Wagnalls, 1974

Malone, Maggie, *Classic American Patchwork Quilt Patterns*. New York: Sterling Publishing Company, 1979

McKim, Ruby, *One Hundred & One Patchwork Patterns*. New York: Dover Publications, 1962

Pforr, Effie Chalmers, *Award Winning Quilts*. Birmingham, Ala.: Oxmoor House, Inc., 1974

Risinger, Hettie, *Innovative Machine Quilting*. New York: Sterling Publishing Company, 1980

Safford, Carleton L. and Bishop, Robert, *America's Quilts and Coverlets*. Barre, Mass.: Weathervane Books, 1974

PERIODICALS

Quilt World, House of White Birches

Quilt, Harris Publications

Ladies Circle Patchwork Quilts

Quilter's Newsletter, Leman Publications

Index

INDEX

Number enclosed in parentheses is the number of the design. The second number is the page number.